Quiet

Hearing God Amidst The Noise

AJ Sherrill

Copyright © 2014 AJ Sherrill

All rights reserved.

ISBN: 149522550X
ISBN 13: 9781495225505
Library of Congress Control Number: 2014901097
CreateSpace Independent Publishing Platform
North Charleston, South Carolina

*By waiting and calm you shall be saved,
In quiet and trust lies your strength.*
-Isaiah 30:15b

Contents

INTRODUCTION	[Why] this Matters	1
1 NOISE	[What] is the Crisis?	5
2 ROOM	[Where] God Dwells	15
3 STILL	[What] Should Be	23
4 GROANS	[Who] Lives Within	37
5 DIVE	[How] to Pray	47
6 GAZE	[When] You Know You're Known	55
BIBLIOGRAPHY		65

INTRODUCTION

If these words could descend from my head into my heart and become part of my innermost self, I would be a converted man.
-HENRI M. NOUWEN[1]

WHY THIS MATTERS

Every moment of every day the most significant reality in the entire universe is the radical availability of God's Presence. Yet, in almost every moment of every day we remain unaware of this generous gift. One of the ways our Christian ancestors experienced this gift is through contemplation. For the purpose of this work, contemplation is simply "the practice of stilling ourselves before God, moving ever deeper into the core of our being and simply offering ourselves to God in totally vulnerable love."[2] Contemplative spirituality may be the most challenging of all the practices in Christian discipleship. We know Jesus spent 40 days in the wilderness before uttering the most

1. Henri M. Nouwen, *The Genesee Diary*, 32-33.
2. M. Robert Mulholland Jr., *The Deeper Journey,* 97.

unconventional wisdom the world had ever heard (the *Beatitudes*). No one can spend 40 straight days thinking and talking. Prayer must become more for us than thinking thoughts and saying words to God. We simply run out of things to say. At some point our relationship with God demands we move away from words, away from noise, and away from the mental chatter toward discovering God in the quiet, the stillness and the silence. This little book is about how we begin to do that.

I recently watched the movie, *Gravity*. Throughout the film the juxtaposition between earth and space is stark. Whereas earth is portrayed as noisy, busy and full of agendas, space is depicted as silent, void and timeless. *Gravity* is an action film to be sure, but I found it as equally haunting as it was thrilling. Half way through the film, for me, came the climax. The lead character, played by Sandra Bullock, was threatened with the prospect of death as she uttered an unforgettable confession:

I'd pray but no one ever taught me how.

An irony in the church today is that many profess a deep spirituality while, at the same time, confess a shallow prayer life. To borrow a phrase from Scripture, "My *brothers* and sisters, this *should not be*."[3] It really can't be, in fact. There is no such thing as a dynamic spirituality without a healthy prayer life because spirituality is intimacy with God through prayer.

---

3. 2. James 3:10

When asked to define one's prayer life many point only to words they speak to God, and impressions they claim to feel from God. Whereas this is a form of prayer, it only begins to scratch the surface of God's depth in relationship. This resource is designed to introduce the practice of stillness, silence and being as a mode of prayer. Many Protestants are particularly unfamiliar with this practice, and sometimes understandably so, as contemplation is often conflated with Eastern Religion, which omits the necessity of receiving the Spirit of God through the work of Christ's life, death, resurrection, and ascension. I pray this little book will challenge, encourage and inspire you to reconnect with the most significant happening in the universe at every moment: God's abiding Presence.

1

NOISE

*But the LORD was not in the wind.
And after the wind an earthquake,
But the LORD was not in the earthquake.
And after the earthquake a fire,
But the LORD was not in the fire.
And after the fire the sound of a low whisper.*
-1 KINGS 19:11-12

WHAT IS THE CRISIS?

I live in Manhattan, the city where noise doesn't sleep. Sirens are our soundtrack. Every evening my avenue jams with irritated drivers lining up to enter the thin gates of the Lincoln Tunnel. Their aggravated negotiations send an unwelcome cacophony of perpetual horns through my windows. And this symphony sounds more like the novice of a middle school band than the genius of a city orchestra.

A few blocks north, tourists walk the gauntlet of advertising, also known as Times Square, where the lights are bright as day in the dead of night. Bordering my apartment is a park called The Highline, where neighbors and visitors stroll along speaking every language imaginable. Manhattan is like a modern day Babel only with many towers and equally as many tongues. After two years in the city, my wife and I welcomed a baby girl into our family, and she voices her needs around the clock. In sum, the sheer decibels of life have never been higher. I need to read this book as much as anybody.

New York City has long been known for the clamor of its streets, but research supports that noise pollution is on the rise. A study showed that in 1968 it took 15 hours to record one hour of pure nature without the ambient sounds of airplanes, cars and other manufactured reverberations. As of the year 2005, it took more than 2000 hours of recorded time to yield the same hour of pure nature sounds.[4] As more and more of the world's population moves to cities, I'd say our lives are not wanting for noise.

The tragedy in all of this is that our prayers often imitate the flow of the city. If you are like me, the sum total of prayer is often:
TALKING
READING
THINKING
PETITIONING
CONFESSING

---

4. http://stmartins.co.za/documents/nooma/noise.pdf

And so on and so forth.

And when I run out of matters to say or things to think, it's time to move on to the next item on the day's schedule. I'm imaging what my wife would think if this were the extent of "conversation" with her. It would render her voice mute. It reduces relationship to monologue, and that's not much of a relationship. Many outwardly boast of a robust prayer life, but are inwardly anxious, chatty and bored. If you find yourself resonating with this confession thus far, this book is for you.

Seeking the Silence

In the early 18th century, Madame Jeanne Guyon, a prayer warrior from France, wrote about the revolution of silence in her prayer life. She longed to see those young in faith "make a transition from anxious striving to stillness and pure trust in God."[5] Her instruction was to cultivate a prayer life that was far more passive than active, more still than busy, and more desirous to listen than to speak. Although I would not have admitted it, the constant chatter and inner noise in my prayer life was a form of striving that I called "prayer."

Now, before you think I view prayer as one big, silent sit, let me say that we do in fact need to talk, read, think, petition and confess as a part of our prayer life. This type of prayer is called "cataphatic" spirituality. We will get to that later. But my assumption is that you are already doing

---
5. (2009-07-16). Christian Spirituality: The Classics (p. 266). Taylor and Francis. Kindle Edition.

this. So, rather than reinforcing what you already do so well, I hope to plant a tiny seed in your soul that seeking God in the silence is perhaps the missing dimension from your prayer life.

But how do we go about seeking silence amidst all this noise? Must we leave the city, hire a babysitter, or retreat to the monastery every time we desire to pray this way? Martin Laird, a professor of theology at Villanova University, asserts that a sound-proof environment isn't a prerequisite for silent prayer. In fact, he explains, fixating on noise often only creates more noise in our thinking.

> Coping with disruptive noise that we simply cannot do anything about does not so much call for praying [for] noise reduction as for being resolved that it's okay for the noise to be there if nothing can be done about it. To get caught up in a buzzing commentary on how irritating the noise is makes for a noisy relationship with noise... First, we are in a position to learn something from silence and its generous way of allowing noise to be present when it happens to be present. To get caught up in commentary on the noise will not make it go away but will only tighten the clenching of our jaws around our preference that the noise be gone. Silence is wide and gracious enough to allow sound, even irritating sound, to be present. Second, instead of trying to push disruption away, we shift our attention away from the

disrupting noise to our prayer word or to whatever
our contemplative practice is.[6]

Getting hung up on the presence of noise is one of myriad ways the inner noise of the mind can be just as loud as the sirens on my street, and this inner noise is harder to shake than taking a train ride out of the city. The practice of contemplative prayer teaches us to silence noise no matter the context. It begins with "nothing more than to meet the noise with stillness and not commentary."[7] Your inner commentary adds to the noise from which we are seeking freedom. Our intimacy with God depends on it.

Inner Noise

Psychologist, author, and science journalist, Daniel Goleman contends "there are two main varieties of distractions: sensory and emotional."[8] Having dealt the external, sensory distractions above we now turn within to the emotional, internal noise. Several years ago, aware of the constant inner noise of my mind, I took a day at a nearby monastery. I had diagnosed the problem of noise (both outer and inner), but had yet to learn the skill of silence. Arriving early on a cold, January morning, I sat patiently and expectantly in the sanctuary as the monks in their

---

6. Laird, Martin (2011-06-29). A Sunlit Absence: Silence, Awareness, and Contemplation (p. 50). Oxford University Press. Kindle Edition.

7. Ibid., 56.

8. Goleman, Daniel (2013-10-08). Focus: The Hidden Driver of Excellence (p. 14). HarperCollins. Kindle Edition.

"habits" (monastic robes) chanted in unison. They completed their sunrise service and slowly vacated the space. The room was still and silent, yet, I found the inner chatter of my mind deafening. I had come for peace, but after 2 hours I was only more aware of the war in my mind. Dejectedly, I got up and left. I simply had no idea how to silence the inner monologue.

According to St. Hesychios (8th century), the mind is like "a donkey going round and round in a mill, and cannot step out of the circle to which it is tethered."[9] Even when the outer noise is muted the inner chatter continues. The three chief triggers perpetuating this cycle are:

COMPETENCE
COMPARISON
CONTROL

When we are sill enough, it is embarrassing how insecure we become about our perceived competency. We obsess with questions like:
Am I good enough?
Can I sustain this level of output?

In the absence of noise, the mind questions how we compare to those around us.
Are they better than me?
Am I as smart as they?

---

9. Laird, Martin (2011-06-29). A Sunlit Absence: Silence, Awareness, and Contemplation (p. 73). Oxford University Press. Kindle Edition.

When the external sounds around us fade, we ponder questions of control like:

Is my future secure?

How might I achieve this or that desired outcome?

These conversations dominate the mind.

What we come to find in life is not so much that we are creating thoughts, but that our thoughts are creating us. And like a donkey, we go around and around, unable to get off the mill. In the end, the mind is a magnificent servant and a horrendous master. Laird again contends,

> In early seasons of practice… when we try to be silent we find that there is anything but silence. This inner noise is generated by a deeply ingrained tendency, reinforced over a lifetime, to derive our sense of who we are and what our life is about from these thoughts and feelings. We look within and genuinely think that we are our thoughts and feelings. If our thoughts and feelings were a mass of vines and branches, we would say we were smack in the middle of it all. In fact, we might even say that we were this tangle of vines.[10]

We derive far too much of our identity from the inner chatter of our heads. Descartes was wrong. We do not know we exist because we think with our brains. Our

---
10. Ibid., 17.

existence includes thinking but is not wholly defined by it. At the monastery, this much became clear: Tragically, my mind was the determining script of my heart, soul and will—and I had very little control over it. This needed balance; I needed breakthrough. Only months later did I discover our spiritual ancestors understood this reality and developed tools to move deeply into silence. And in the silence God met them.

Practice

This week pay close attention to the first place your mind veers when you wake up (e.g. email, anxiety, Scripture, finances, a relationship, etc.). These initial directions often reveal from where you draw identity.

Let's begin the practice of seeking God in the silence in the "shallow end of the pool." Resist the temptation to dive too deeply too quickly. Beginners are often tempted to prematurely jettison the path due to frustration, perceiving a lack of results. But learning silent prayer is like starting a new exercise program—you have to learn to use new muscles, which always feels awkward and unproductive at first.

In the sixth century, Saint Benedict developed a meditative approach to Scripture reading called *lectio divina* (Latin for "divine reading"). This method prioritizes what God is *speaking* to us just as much as what God *spoke* to our ancestors. In other words, *lectio divina* invites the Holy Spirit into the reading as it moves the reader in four distinct directions: READ, MEDITATE, PRAY, CONTEMPLATE

So as not to get bogged down with new terminology, follow this simple pathway in your Scripture reading today:

1) Create an inviting/inspiring space. Perhaps this means lighting a candle, tidying a room, creating a playlist to underscore, and sitting in your favorite chair.

2) Select a passage to read from Scripture.

3) Have paper/journal and a pen handy.

4) Give yourself to these four directions (20 minutes total, 5 minutes for each).

    a. READ – Slowly read the selected text 3 times.

    b. REFLECT – Select a word or phrase off the page that sticks out.

    c. WRITE – Spend time writing about why you selected that word or phrase.

    d. REST – Suspend all thought and sit quietly with God. Trust that God heard your worry, anxiety and/or longings, and is acting on your behalf (Romans 8:28).

2

Room

*But when you pray, go into your room and shut the door
and pray to your Father who is in secret.*
-Jesus of Nazareth[11]

Where God Dwells

In the greatest sermon ever heard, Jesus breaks down authentic spirituality into the three central practices: give, pray, fast. Volumes have been written on each practice. For the purposes of this work, Jesus' instruction on prayer warrants our attention. Not only does Jesus guide the disciples in *how* to pray (this is what Christians refer as the "Lord's Prayer") but first he shows them *where* to pray. The Jewish ritual system gathered the people to pray in the synagogue three times per day. Jesus never renounced this public practice, but he advocated for private prayer as well.

---

11. Matthew 6:6, ESV.

Over time, it can be tempting to let public worship dominate one's spiritual life while neglecting personal intimacy cultivated with God through prayer. The Sermon on the Mount is the only place in Scripture where God commands us to pray in private. A group of devout Christ followers in the third century C.E., called the Desert Fathers, believed solitude was essential for discipleship. There was a saint at that time called Abba Moses. One day, a brother came to him asking where to find wisdom. Abba Moses echoed Jesus' instruction saying, "Go and sit in your cell, and your cell will teach you everything."[12] Matthew records Jesus' use of *tameion* (room, pantry, closet) to refer to the place where one is called to meet alone with God. I suggest this word usage carries at least two meanings.

One is an EXTERNAL GEOGRAPHY.
The other is an INTERNAL ANATOMY.

Let's begin with **external geography**. In 1st century dwellings, the common family did not live in a house with many rooms. In fact, most rooms were shared spaces. Therefore, a robust private life was a luxury few could afford. Many scholars believe Jesus was referring to a kitchen-like pantry. This room was often located in the center of a dwelling, devoid of windows. It was here that a family stored dry goods. Praying in this room would ensure

---

12. Gerald Sittser, *Water from a Deep Well*, 83.

privacy, intimacy, and possibly a snack if one's prayer persisted through the better part of the morning. It would promote a couple of things:

1) Sincerity
   This chapter begins with Matthew recording Jesus' caution of hypocrisy. Hypocrisy (Greek: hypokrites) is to act with a mask on; to be a false self, describing a pretentious person.[13]

2) Privacy
   Devoid of windows, there was little possibility of being seen. This reduced the temptation to pray with improper motives.

Later in chapter six, Matthew records Jesus using this same term for "room" (*tameion*) when referring to the birds: "they do not store or reap, they have no *tameion* or barn, yet God feeds them."[14] This usage would support the interpretation of "pantry" or "storage room" in a home as the geographical location to pray in private.

However, there is another dimension to the term that should be explored, and that is the **internal anatomy** within us. When Jesus taught, he often spoke on many levels at once. It was a dynamic feature of his brilliant teaching ministry, which is lucid in his parables. It is plausible that Jesus was teaching his disciples to not only enter an

---

13. Harrington, 94.
14. Matthew 6:26.

external geographical location in the home when praying, but also to enter an internal place in their anatomy; namely, the deepest part of themselves. In other words, he was inviting them to delve into the depths of the soul where the image of God is imprinted, and where the Holy Spirit would dwell after Pentecost.

Gerald Sittser, theologian and author of, *Water from a Deep Well,* rightly states, "involvement in the world has its place, for God calls us to serve the world. But we need distance and quiet too, or the busyness, noise, demands and pressures of the world will consume us."[15] Finding a pantry in your life is essential. Consider where this sacred place lies for you to regularly meet with God. It could be a room, an office, a chair, a church, or wherever you can rest and seek God in the silence.

The haunting challenge to the Christian is whether or not we are entering into our own depths when we go to God in prayer. Perhaps this explains the chronic boredom in prayer many claim to experience. It is far too easy to launch shallow prayers in God's direction on the way out the door. This is illustrated in the Epistle of James when he addressed the scattered church "who do not have because they do not ask."[16] And when they do ask, they do not receive because their prayers are in alignment with the flesh and not God's will. James is referring to people who avoid the hard work of entering the external and internal

---

15. Sittser, 83.
16. James 4:2-3.

pantry, sitting long enough to discover who they really are, and what they really want.

Our prayer lives are often overly entrenched by hurry, worry, and circumstance that we rarely consider, let alone pray from the deepest core of who we are. We pray the top of our minds, and our minds are wrapped up in daily dramas and cyclical monologues. That is not to say God is disinterested in our dramas. Far from it, actually. But the peace God gives within our circumstances most often comes in connecting with God in our deepest room, and recognizing that many of the dramas we think urgent are rather fleeting, transitory and meaningless. It is when we move into the depths of the soul that the peace of God can really to meet us. It is there that we realize everything is more than OK.

Jesus' invitation is to seek out an internal monastery within ourselves. Martin Laird said it best: "The only monastery we all need to enter is the one Jesus opened up as he disclosed the inner depths of his own identity and purpose: 'I and the Father are one' (Jn 10:30)."[17] To obey Jesus' command, we don't have to add another room to our houses because the room is already fashioned inside our bodies. The inner room is the soul. And Jesus commands us to go there and pray.

---

17. Laird, Martin (2011-06-29). A Sunlit Absence: Silence, Awareness, and Contemplation (pp. 40-41). Oxford University Press. Kindle Edition.

A Deeper Path

There is yet another dimension of the spiritual life to clarify before moving forward. The dominant meta-narrative of our post-modern world, from which we unconsciously derive our worldview, denies the existence of the mystical and metaphysical. Therefore, reality, for the average person today, is limited to the physical universe. Philosopher, Charles Taylor, calls this the "imminent frame." This means that all we see, touch, taste, hear, and feel is all there is. In this worldview, life is reduced to what we can sense and measure scientifically. While science is undoubtedly useful as a tool, as a worldview it breeds cynicism and hopelessness.

Jesus invited us to explore a deeper reality. Have you ever noticed the way Jesus refers to His parables? Reminding His disciples of the prophet Isaiah, he said, "I speak to them in parables, because seeing they do not see, and hearing they do not hear."[18] The Gospels frequently record Jesus instructing His followers to hear and see at two levels. The first is the cognitive level, where we process, sift, and analyze what has been said or encountered. This often acts as a filter, either accepting or rejecting a claim, and explains why many disbelieve or attempt to explain away the Kingdom of God. The scientific worldview is the dominant filter through which we in the Western hemisphere evaluate what is and is not possible from as early as primary school.

---

18. Matthew 13:13.

The second level is the spiritual, where we evaluate a claim and after affirming it as cognitively plausible, empower the claim to have a transformative effect upon us. Seldom do we get to this level because we are too frightened to deconstruct the false foundations on which our cognitive reasoning frequently stands. Furthermore, spiritual learning regularly strikes such a blow to the constructed ego that most are not prepared to receive it. Thus, time and again in Scripture and today, many walk away from Jesus sad and/or unchanged.

Consider this: Christ invites us to go beyond hearing to really hear—to go beyond seeing in order to see. In other words, there are ever-deeper realms into which we are called to commune with God and gain more understanding. I am not referring to a pseudo-gnostic understanding, only given to the elite and privileged few. I am talking about those who want to move beyond superficial spirituality, which is often contaminated with individualism, consumerism, cognition, and safety. When we move beyond superficial spirituality we enter into the depths of a pool whose bottom always remains abysmal.

This invitation to hear and see is the invitation of contemplative spirituality. Like two mirrors on opposite walls, the reflection into deeper and deeper images never ceases. This is the spirituality we are invited into. It is not a spirituality that boasts, "I get God." But one that confesses, "God has me." It is not a spirituality that closes the imagination, but opens it up. It transforms prayer from talking to God to a practice of being *with* God.

Practice

Father Thomas Keating introduced a term called "centering prayer" to describe the practice that leads one into the inner room of the soul. Throughout this resource, centering prayer will be utilized as a practice to usher you deeper into prayer.

Find a quiet and comfortable place to sit. Rest both feet on the floor so as not to restrict blood flow. Select a word/phrase that you can connect with your breathing. This should not be a long word or phrase because you are going to pair it with your inhalation and exhalation. For example, if your phrase is "come, Lord Jesus" then inhale the word "come," exhale, "Lord Jesus." This word/phrase is not used to focus on. Nor is it overly special in any sense. Rather, it is used to keep the mind from wandering off into subconscious chatter. Feel free to leave the word/phrase if you find stillness easy for you. If your mind wanders, gently return to the word/phrase. When you realize your mind has wandered an important thing to remember is to simply return to your word and into stillness. Don't beat yourself up, or analyze why you lost your way.

Set a timer for ten minutes and breathe in and out with your word/phrase, eventually letting yourself rest in silence, returning to your word as needed. After ten minutes reflect on the experience in your journal.

3

STILL

O God, let me climb through the barriers of sound
And pass into your silence;
And then, in stillness and silence
Let me adore You,
Who are Life-Light-Love
Without beginning and without end.[19]
-SISTER RUTH

WHAT SHOULD BE

Stillness is the forgotten teacher within a society of perpetual movement. Movement means busyness, busyness leads to production, and production yields a bottom line, which in a capitalist society is often our highest ideal. This trajectory is no longer a slice of the pie chart called life; it is the whole pie. Furthermore, this plays out beyond economics and is the

---

19. Sister Ruth, *Oxford Book of Prayer*, edited, 8.

formula we use for our social and spiritual lives as well. And so the zeitgeist of our time is *don't slow down*. We feel the constant urge to produce and we long for instant gratification. In that kind of world it is no wonder that stillness is perceived as an opportunity cost. After all, time is money, right? Ultimately, our addiction to immediacy tempts us to settle for accessible substitutes rather than waiting for what we really long for. Stillness is the gift, resourcing us to zoom out of life, scan the horizon, and discover what it is we *really* long for.

Several months ago I attended a conference, which in and of itself isn't unusual. Having attended dozens of conferences, I have identified their function, by and large, as those places we briefly populate to cherry pick new ideas, borrow concepts, and develop new constructs of production. This is true of conferences in every industry (business, church, technology, education, and so on), and can have a profound impact. But this conference was different, and perhaps that was what compelled me. This one rejected production, construction and idea generation, and honed in on cultivating Divine intimacy through the practice of subtraction. Assessing the frenetic trajectory of my life, it was time for me to hear what this conference had to impart.

It was shocking from the start. Wrongly assuming I would be one of few interested in this conversation, the place was packed. Arriving late so as to not seem too eager, I sat in the last seat remaining – in the back on the far wall. The speaker sat behind a little table, so dwarfed by the size of the room that his image was projected on screens so that the nosebleed section had a visual.

Delicately releasing my bag to the floor, I unzipped the chamber holding my computer and created a fresh document. There I sat, recording with stealth-like ferocity the musings of the speaker behind the table who was dropping morsels of rare wisdom. In short, he was verbally on fire! In between sentences you could hear a pin drop. Only those around me experienced that pin as clatter from my keyboard. A forthright woman next to me leaned over, and not so gently whispered, "Would you mind putting your computer away?" It was more of a statement than a question, really. Recalibrating this odd request, I returned the computer to my bag and again scanned the room. I was one of two people among thousands who bothered to bring a computer, and, as far as I could tell, was one of five not drawing social security checks. Why was this room so old?

During lunch hour I curiously stumbled into conversations with strangers, inquisitive as to why they had come. After half a dozen conversations I put it all together. Humans eventually come to a place of feeling over-produced and exhausted from decades of life construction. We wonder what it is all supposed to mean. And in dire need of subtracting the minutia of life, in our latter years we seek new perspectives to find meaning. And it is not that the construction of our lives is wrong, but that it always over-promises and under-delivers. As Father Richard Rohr espoused in his work, *Falling Upward*, we need this construction in the "first half of life" to awake to what we really long for in the second. Like house hoarders, we have filled our brains with decades of information for which we will find no use later in life. In fact, the cognitive overload, which often weighs us down, crowds out what really matters. Can you relate?

These people were at the conference to learn the art of addition by subtraction. They had heard it all, done it all, and concluded that self-fulfillment and/or God is not "out there" waiting to be accessed. As Saint Augustine said, "Why do you want to speak and not want to listen? You are always rushing out of doors but are unwilling to return into your own house. Your teacher is within."[20] For the Christian, the secret of spirituality is that God (and self-fulfillment) waits to be discovered within the inner room, and stillness is one of the primary pathways inviting us into divine intimacy.

MODES OF SPIRITUALITY

Western Christianity, particularly the Protestant Tradition (of which I am a part), has largely emphasized *cataphatic* spirituality nearly to the exclusion of *apophatic* spirituality. Together they form two imperative sides of the same coin. Cataphatic is a compound word roughly meaning "descend" and "speak." When combined the word describes the endeavor "to bring God down in such a way so as to speak of God."[21] Again, this is a necessary mode. Cynthia Bourgeault defines cataphatic spirituality as

---

20. Saint Augustine, Exposition on Psalm 139, chap. 15, in Expositions on the Psalms, trans. M. Boulding (Hyde Park, N.Y.: New City Press, 2004), 297.
21. http://www.merriam-webster.com/word-of-the-day/2010/09/26.

> prayer that makes use of what theologians call our 'faculties.' It engages our reason, memory, imagination, feeling and will. These are the normal human operating systems that connect us with the outer world and to our own interior life… they are wonderful tools… Cataphatic prayer is most of what we are about in church.[22]

This mode of spirituality is satisfied by the fruit of progress. Developing theology, hearing a "word" from God, memorizing Scripture, seeing visions, singing songs, making confession and accessing clarity are all meaningful activities within cataphatic spirituality. The other (often neglected) side of the coin is *apophatic* spirituality. Bourgeault describes apophasis as that which

> bypasses our capacities for reason, imagination, visualization, emotion and memory… It, too, makes use of faculties, but ones that are much more subtle than we're used to and which are normally blocked by over-reliance on our more usual mental processing modes.[23]

Whereas the cataphatic is satisfied with doing/knowing, the apophatic is satisfied with being. Both belong, yet we must be intent to recover the one that has been lost.

---

22. Cynthia Bourgeault, *Centering Prayer and Inner…* 32.
23. Ibid.

This is precisely where we subvert the noise of life, enter the inner room, and move into stillness.

This mode of spirituality is unappealing to many in our post-modern society because it is ostensibly unproductive by nature. Dietrich Bonhoeffer provides a helpful defense to this inaccurate assumption: "To be silent does not mean to be inactive; rather it means to breathe in the will of God, to listen attentively and be ready to obey."[24] If Jesus did only what He saw the Father doing (John 5:19), how are we to perceive God's present activity if our hearts are busy, and not still? Furthermore, God's "activity" is often to sit with us and not to get us to do something that would falsely serve as a force of meaning outside of God's Presence. When you think about these two modes of spirituality, which side do you have a tendency to over-emphasize? How does that inform your pursuit of God this week?

Directions Of Prayer

Within a spiritual climate that often avoids the apophatic, it is inadequate to talk about the problem without moving into practical steps toward it. I have met many who long for a quieter life with God, a stiller soul of peace, and freedom from the pervasive inner chatter, but feel it remains elusive. When I teach on stillness and rest in the church, particularly in urban contexts, I visibly observe weary eyes focus and postures straighten. We are tired, longing for respite. To clarify what a step toward the

---

24. Bonhoeffer, Dietrich (2012-09-28). God Is on the Cross: Reflections on Lent and Easter (p. 8). Westminster John Knox Press. Kindle Edition.

apophatic would look like, there are four helpful directions of prayer to help us identify where we are and how to move into a more balanced spirituality.

In his work, *Armchair Mystics*, Mark Thibodeaux describes these four directions utilizing prepositions as their line of demarcation:

Talking AT God
Talking TO God
Listening TO God
Being WITH God[25]

Talking at God is what many children learn beside their beds at night. Folding little hands and bending miniature knees, simple phrases are launched toward the sky in hopes of Divine reception. As we mature, we develop our own language with God, a kind of conversational tone. This is what Thibodeaux describes as talking to God. You can easily tell in a prayer group who has practiced cataphatic prayer and who has not. There is often ease with the word selection they use in prayer. Many even have a preferred way to address God (e.g. Father, Jesus, Lord, etc., and I even hear Daddy from time to time). Many who are new to prayer refresh us with their simplicity as they begin early stage prayer (talking at God) later in life. The listening to God phase of prayer is a mark of maturity where one comes to discover that the relationship is both give and take. It is no

---
25. Mark Thibodeaux, *Armchair Mystics*, 17.

different in human relationships, which flourish only when both speak and listen in turn. Thibodeaux asserts, "This is often felt by receiving an impression from God, an image that leads us further into something, and/or a word that clarifies what we have been needing to hear or know."[26] All three of these directions are cataphatic in nature. Although the third direction moves us into listening, it is still dependent on images, feelings and words. To reiterate, these directions are good, but incomplete. They are comfortable, but lacking. Activist, Carlo Carretto wisely said, "This is crucial: as long as we pray only when and how we want to, our life of prayer is bound to be unreal."[27]

The fourth direction, often omitted and uncomfortable, is being with God. This stage, Thibodeaux contends,

> is radically different from all the others for two reasons. First, it is not an action like talking or listening, but rather is a state of being. It is not so much what I do during my prayer times, but who I've become because of them. Second, because this is not an action that I can do, it is virtually out of my control. Unlike the other stages, I cannot make this stage happen. It must come as a pure gift from God. All I can do is till the soil so that the land

---

26. Ibid.

27. Carretto, Carlo (2012-08-01). Letters from the Desert (Anniversary Edition) (Kindle Locations 270-271). Orbis Books. Kindle Edition.

will be fertile when the Sower comes to plant the seeds.[28]

This is the all-important stage of surrendering the outcome in prayer. No longer do you need to demand God "show up" for you in a certain way such as a feeling, impression, or word of clarity. It is enough to be with God in this form of prayer. Like Mary, in this phase we treasure God in our hearts knowing that is enough. Stillness is the great, lost teacher of our time.

Is It Biblical?

When I first began to detect a longing in my soul for this way of connecting with God I questioned its Biblical veracity. Perhaps you do too. I affirm the impulse to question contemplative spirituality as it (like every other discipline) has been abused and misrepresented at times. Further, it is utilized in other religious and non-religious traditions in ways that are far different from Christian orthodoxy. But rather than write it off because of the way it has been misused, let's become curious as to whether we can see this pattern in Jesus. L. Paul Jensen's work, *Subversive Spirituality*, brilliantly displays moments in the Gospels where Jesus slips away to be with God. Consider the following:

---

28. Thibodeaux S.J., Mark (2011-08-09). Armchair Mystic: Easing into Contemplative Prayer (p. 29). St. Anthony Messenger Press. Kindle Edition.

Event — Reference

The Temptation.......Matthew 4:1-11, Mark 1:11-13, Luke 4:1-13

Early Morning
Prayer ....Mark 1:35, Luke 4:42

Pattern of
Withdrawal............Luke 5:16

Retreating with
Disciples ....Matthew 5-7

Away for rest ....Matthew 14:13, Mark 6:30-32, Luke 9:10

Evening Prayer........Matthew 14:22-33, Mark 6:45-52

The Transfiguration..Matthew 17:1-13, Mark 9:2-13, Luke 9:28-36

Last Supper............Matthew 26:17-30, Mark 14:12-26, Luke 22:14-39

Gethsemane...........Matthew 26:36-46, Mark 14:32-42, Luke 22:39-46[29]

In Jesus' wilderness temptation, one could reasonably conclude that Jesus didn't talk at/with God for 40 days straight. Moreover, in the stillness He observed what the Father was doing and responded to Satan in the way He did as a result. Succinctly put, Jesus knew the value of stilling the soul, away from the crowd, as a resource equipping Him to return effectively to the crowd. He lived a life that first valued the inner room before endeavoring an outward ministry.

---

29. L. Paul Jensen, *Subversive Spirituality*, 86-87.

Driving home his point, Jensen legitimizes his case from the world of social media:

> Social media is an outlet to live life incessantly directed toward the world. We continuously "check in" to give and receive messages to and from the world. It is perpetual information acquisition. Even when we leave "the world" and return home for the evening, we are still oriented toward the crowd. But Jesus often oriented life away from the crowd. Jesus never "checked in" with the crowd. He only found himself in the crowd after being empowered from solitude. Consider the following, outlining Jesus' commitment to withdrawing to be with God and the disciples.[30]

In agreement with Thibodeaux's observation, Martin Laird avers,

> One of the early realizations of the life of stillness is that the opposite of the contemplative life is not the active life but the reactive life: highly habituated emotional styles and lifestyles that keep us constantly reacting to life like victimizing victims, ever more convinced that the videos that dominate and shape our awareness are in fact true. The life of stillness gradually heals this split

---

30. Ibid., 86.

and leads us into wide-open fields where buried treasure lies (Mt 13:45–46), fields where the soul can bathe in its own space and make long swathes in meadow lengths of space. The God we seek already shines through our eyes. May our seeking not blind us to what already lies hidden in plain sight all around us.[31]

Stillness is a great teacher. In a society of noise, we must again take it seriously if we are to fully return to who God believes we are.

Once I understood the Biblical support for contemplation, I then questioned its usefulness. Perhaps this is where you are too. Lest we become too anti-production, if stillness were entirely useless, what would be the point? Thankfully, the fruits of cultivating stillness are greater self and God awareness, and increased clarity about life. The Greek mystic, Saint Diadochus likens the mind to the sea:

> When the sea is calm, fishermen can scan its depths and therefore hardly any creature moving in the water escapes their notice. But when the sea is disturbed by the winds it hides beneath its turbid and agitated waves what it was happy to reveal when it was smiling and calm; and then the fishermen's skill

---
31. Laird, Martin (2011-06-29). A Sunlit Absence: Silence, Awareness, and Contemplation (p. 42). Oxford University Press. Kindle Edition.

and cunning prove vain. The same thing happens with the contemplative power of the intellect.[32]

The problem isn't that the waters of life are murky. The problem is that they are raging. Once we diagnose that reality, stillness permits us to quiet them. And as we quiet the tides of the mind we can begin to see clearly to the bottom, recognizing who we are and what we are after. According to Laird, when we still ourselves,

> The ocean depth of awareness can be gazed into. This is the invitation of interior silence. We look right into the mind, right into awareness itself in which thoughts and feelings appear and disappear, whether they are like troubled, stormy waters or feathery ocean foam.[33]

There is a reason that being with God is an often omitted practice in our time. Stillness requires discipline. And not only is this pathway of discipline biblical, it is also historic. Henri Nouwen defined this discipline as "the effort to create some space in which God can act."[34] Evagrius of Ponticus believed, "the practice of stillness is full of joy and beauty."[35] Even Bonhoeffer believed it essential, "we

---

32. Ibid., 60.

33. Ibid.

34. Henri Nouwen, *Moving from Solitude to Community to Ministry*, Leadership Journal, Spring 1995, 81.

35. Laird, 43.

are silent early in the morning because God should have the first word, and we are silent before going to bed because the last word also belongs to God."[36] Truly, it is in the stillness that we still the sea of the soul long enough to become aware of what we really need. This practice of prayer is hard, requiring discipline and intention otherwise everyone would do it.

PRACTICE

Return again to the practice of centering prayer. This time set the time for twelve minutes. Afterwards, record observations about the experience in your journal.

---

36. Dietrich Bonhoeffer, *Life Together,* 85.

4

GROANS

Likewise the Spirit helps us in our weakness. For we do not know what to pray for as we ought, but the Spirit himself intercedes for us with groanings too deep for words. And he who searches hearts knows what is the mind of the Spirit, because the Spirit intercedes for the saints according to the will of God.
-PAUL, THE APOSTLE (ROMANS 8:26-27)

WHO LIVES WITHIN

Paul writes that *we do not know what to pray for as we ought*. "We" is that part of us we most often identify — the "surface" self, if you will. Although that part of us is a piece of who we are, it is not our deepest, truest identity. Therefore, when we identify most with the part of ourselves Paul referred to, we never pray from the deeper rooms within (chapter 2).

In 2007 I moved from pastoring a community in Central Florida to planting a church in Southern California. Everything about church planting one needs to know, but soon forgets, lies in the term itself: *church planting*. The vocation requires the patience of a farmer rather than the efficiency of a machinist. Fictitious deadlines, fundraising, and chronic comparison tragically derail church "planters" into church "mechanics." Several months into the project, I needed a breakthrough. Only I was unaware of what form my breakthrough would take.

Pertinently, around that time a friend was hosting a workshop centered on the life and ministry of Henri Nouwen. Nouwen had left his teaching position at Yale to serve and learn from the mentally handicapped in a community called *Daybreak*. His life had been characterized by the same competency, compare, and control merry-go-round as mine (and perhaps yours).

While attending this workshop I went to lunch with a man whom I'd met that morning. We were discussing the pressures of life and the desire to connect more deeply with God. It is often difficult to reconcile the depth of our ancestors faith with the superficiality characterized by much of Western Christianity today. The more we talked, the more I realized this man had developed the disciplines necessary to move beyond talking at God and was growing into being with God. This was the necessary breakthrough I was waiting for. By the end of lunch I was able to articulate what had previously been only an unnamed impression. Not only did I want this kind of relationship with God, but it was in line with the same longings of the early church, the Desert Fathers, the monastic communities and many other traditions along the way.

It occurred to me that maybe it was time to stop circling around the mill in my mind—that maybe there was a better conversation happening within me that I needed to join. This is where Romans 8:26-27 came into play. Marjorie J. Thompson says it well:

> Have you considered what an astonishing promise it is that the Spirit prays in us, and does so 'according to the will of God'? Perhaps our real task in prayer is to attune ourselves to the conversation already going on deep in our hearts. Then we may align our conscious intentions with the desire of God being expressed at our core.[37]

In the passage above Paul rightly confesses that we do, in fact, have weaknesses. Further, the Spirit within every disciple longs to help where we are weak. The problem is that competency, comparison and control are each habitual and subversive strategies to strive in our own capacities. We equate strength with feeling equipped and competent in our abilities. We believe the illusion that comparing ourselves to others can lead to personal victory. We swallow whole the lie that if we can only control our lives through worry, manipulation and working harder then we will get

---

[37]. Marjorie J. Thompson. Soul Feast: An Invitation to the Christian Spiritual Life (Kindle Locations 545-547). Kindle Edition.

what we want. Perhaps these are the very weaknesses from which the Spirit seeks to liberate us.

I believe, in this text, Paul is implying we are so caught up in our inner dramas that we lack the clarity to know what to pray for. That is how lost we are in our heads. To find our way back requires us to pursue the inverse of our impulses:

> stillness,
> silence,
> and surrender

Surrendering to the Holy Spirit, who indwells, connects us to the eternal dialogue within the Trinity – which is a better conversation that the one in our heads. Entering this conversation reminds us of what is real. And the truth is, **we are less important than we think, yet more loved than we know.** The loss of this "significance" is actually a grace because our self-worth no longer has to be defended through competition, comparison and control. What a liberation! Furthermore, the love of God brings us into the deeper mystery of union that Christ unlocked for us. Madame Guyon spoke of the "annihilation" of our perceived significance:

> But is not annihilation a bitter thing? Oh! If only you knew the virtue and the blessing which the soul receives from having passed into this experience.

This is the mystery of surrender: one dies to self, only to 'bear fruit' in unexpected ways. 'Unless a grain of wheat falls into the earth and dies, it remains just a single grain; but if it dies, it bears much fruit' (Jn 12:24).[38]

So May we get off the donkey around the mill and enter the eternal conversation—the joy, and the mystery of what the Holy Spirit is constantly speaking with the Father and the Son. Furthermore, the conversation within the Trinity is full of sacrifice, acceptance and creative love toward the other. Is this not the conversation we prefer to be brought into rather than the inner chatter of critique and ego?

GROANS

Paul says that the Holy Spirit is groaning in us. What does that mean? In this passage, the biblical Greek, *stenagmois* (groanings), clearly refers to the action of the Spirit within us. Scholars have explored what this mysterious expression of the Spirit might be like. Douglas Moo insists the groans of the Spirit are "unspoken, never rising to the audible level at all."[39] Bill Mounce, claims it is "our failure to know God's will and our consequent inability to petition God specifically and assuredly is met by God's Spirit, who Himself expresses to God those intercessory petitions that

---

38. (2009-07-16). *Christian Spirituality: The Classics* (p. 262). Taylor and Francis. Kindle Edition.

39. http://www.teknia.com/blog/who%E2%80%99s-doing-groaning-rom-826 (accessed Nov. 13, 2013).

perfectly match the will of God."[40] The poetry of Sister Ruth from *The Oxford Book of Prayer* illustrates this soundless, nonverbal communion:

> Let me climb through the barriers of sound
> and pass into your silence;
> And then, in stillness and silence
> let me adore You,
> Who are Life-Light-Love-
> Without beginning and without end.[41]

Paul's instruction in Romans 8 is perhaps the strongest admonition in the epistles to quiet the mind and attune the soul to silence. For it is only in the silence that we hear God's whispers of liberation from the burden of establishing and defending our own significance. It has been said God's first language is silence because, through Christ's atonement, God has nothing to say against us. God's silence is, therefore, a divine affirmation of acceptance despite our depraved human condition. Therefore, Romans 8 beckons us into a deeper conversation with God. Rather than viewing prayer as the beginning of a new conversation, it is essential to understand prayer as an invitation to join the conversation that began long ago.

---

40. Ibid.
41. George Appleton. *The Oxford Book of Prayer*. Oxford [Oxfordshire]: Oxford University Press, 1985, 8.

CRITIQUES

One of the rightful criticisms of contemplative prayer is the fear of surrendering into nothingness. Many skeptics have compared contemplation to diving into a pool that may or may not have water to support our fall. Unlike Buddhist meditation into opaque vastness with a goal of desire-lessness, Christian contemplation is a dive into the Holy Spirit who lives and groans within the believer. Rather than falling into nothing, we fall into Someone. The Spirit never calls us to jettison all desire, but does promises to be with us always. Therefore, Christian contemplation is meant to align our desires with God's will. There is no need to fear the descent, for it is the Spirit of Christ who awaits our company and invites us into the conversation.

When I first began praying in this way, both my thoughts and my body fought my efforts to be still. Not only was it necessary to still my racing thoughts, but my body was suddenly alive with pangs and impulses that distracted me. Posture is important. Sitting up in a comfortable position with both feet on the floor so as not to constrict blood flow is the first recommendation. But I often wondered what to do with the chatter in my head.

The Desert Fathers taught that the outward posture of prayer helped form the inward reality. When moving into still and silent prayer, it is helpful to bend one's head toward the heart. This position reflects the priority of the heart informing the mind rather than the other way around. Again, it is not that there is anything wrong with the mind. But for most of our lives the mind is always in the seat of control over all our faculties. If nothing more, this posture serves to balance our approach in prayer. Not only is placing the head into the heart a restful position, but it serves as a continual statement that the heart is steering the ship, and not the mind. Here, Laird refers to Saint Augustine in his work, *The Sunlit Absence*:

> St. Augustine comments on the significance of Christ's resurrection and ascension: Christ 'has gone from our sight so that we should 'return to our heart' (Is 46:8) and find him there.' The heart, a term that refers not to our thoughts and feelings but to our innermost depths that ground thought and feeling, our knowing center, is the place of divine encounter. Just because the Risen Christ is not accessible to the senses in the way the historical Jesus was, this does not imply absence but draws us to a Presence that is deeper than our discursive and imagining powers can perceive, but in which the heart delights.[42]

This position reminds me time and again that the mind submits to the Spirit, who lives within the center of my being. For me, this is a posture of submission to the voice of the Spirit. This is the posture in which I can begin to hear the groans of the Spirit within me intercede according to the will of God.

---

42. Laird, Martin (2011-06-29). A Sunlit Absence: Silence, Awareness, and Contemplation (p. 92). Oxford University Press. Kindle Edition.

Practice

The Eastern Orthodox Church has longed practiced the tradition of meditating on what is known as the "Jesus Prayer." In recent days, the Western Church has found it useful as it is utilized in many denominations. Similar to centering prayer, the Jesus Prayer centers on the phrase:

> Lord Jesus Christ (inhale),
> Son of God (exhale),
> have mercy on me (inhale),
> a sinner (exhale).

This meditational phrase re-centers our identities on the person of Christ. It also acknowledges our inadequacy as sinners apart from the mercy of God. Set your timer for fifteen minutes today and practice this form of prayer. Afterward, record the experience in your journal.

5

DIVE

*By waiting and calm you shall be saved;
in quiet and trust lies your strength*
ISAIAH 30:15

HOW TO PRAY

Martin Laird rightly stated, "Prayer matures by a process of breaking down rather than by acquisition and spiritual prowess."[43] Because our cultural conditioning demands words, objectives, and entertainment, it is helpful when beginning this difficult method of prayer to secure an image to usher you into prayer. This is an image you can return to (just like your word) when you mind takes over. Once you move beyond the entry level of contemplation, you may let go of the image as it will have served its purpose.

---

43. Laird, 90.

Early in my development of this way of prayer, two images have guided me. Although both were useful, I have found one of the images superior to the other.

Image 1 – the inferior: From a birds-eye view I float on a river. This river has a definitive current carrying me downstream. Along the banks of the river I see good things: friends inviting me to a meal, trees providing shade and rest, towns and cities to dock my boat and experience. However, the current of the river flows straight into the heart of Jesus. Although the banks invite me into good things, were I to get off and partake, I would forfeit what is better.

This was the first image I used when beginning contemplation. The good things along the way represented ideas in my head, daily items to attend to, weekend activities, and so on and so forth. Again, these are good things. It was just that these things didn't deserve the contemplative moment of my prayer time. I came to visualize that for the 12 minutes of prayer, it was more useful to stay in the boat and float toward Jesus than get off onto the banks of the daily schedule. Whereas this image was a helpful teacher to let thoughts pass by without commentary or distraction, it was also flawed. This image still oriented my prayers around the production of arriving in the heart of Jesus. It demanded a successful outcome by staying in the boat and getting to the end of the river. I am not saying this is wrong, but misses one of the main thrusts of contemplation: Being, not achieving. Or, to put it another way, surrendering the outcome.

Image 2 – the superior: It is the image of a deep dive into the depths of sea. I begin prayer imagining that I am a diver in the middle of the sea, descending to the bottom. Once I arrive at the bottom I sit on the sea's floor. It is dark, spacious and vacuous. Similarly, Teresa of Avila once said, "The soul is vast, spacious, plentiful."[44]

When I look up I see boats gliding by on the water's surface. These boats represent the chatter of my mind. And I desperately want to see what's in them, where they lead, and what they have to say. I soon discover that I have unintentionally chased the chatter in my mind, and I imagine I've instantaneously returned to the water's surface, peering over the side of a boat. Gently, I release my grip of the boat and descend back to the depths of sea. At the depths of the sea there is nothing to produce, attain, or see. The only thing to do there is to simply be and to wait with God. There I sit patiently in silence, returning to my sacred word. It is enough to be in that moment with God, as I do not need to drift down a current toward a goal or destination. This is what I call, "the dive." It best supports contemplation as a state of being, not doing or achieving. It is helpful to utilize it to begin silent prayer each day.

Distractions tempting us to surface the water are strong, especially at first. My own experience aligns with what Martin Laird said so well:

---

44. Teresa of Avila, Interior Castle 7.1 (trans. Starr, 262).

> The practice of contemplation quiets the noise that goes on in our heads and allows inner silence to expand. This expanding inner silence is a wide and fertile delta that embraces the mud, reeds, and rushes of all sound, whether delightful or disruptive. Initially, however, the practice of contemplation can strike us as frustratingly awkward, and we react to everything within and without. Though we feel drawn to interior silence, what we find when we turn within is a strong headwind of distractions.[45]

When we find ourselves distracted in prayer, caught up in the chatter of the mind, Laird invites us to,

> …simply bring our attention back to our practice whenever we find that our attention has been stolen. The challenge lies in its simplicity. The practice of bringing the attention back time and again creates what is called a habitus or habit, an interior momentum that gradually excavates the present moment, revealing over time the stillness that is within us all like a buried treasure.[46]

What is most important is the grace we give ourselves when we find that we have "surfaced again." God is well aware (and rather patient) with our distracted minds.

---
45. Laird, 22-23.
46. Ibid., 16-17.

When we shift our inner chatter of the day's schedule to shaming ourselves for surfacing to lesser things, we remain disconnected from the depths of the sea. This is the commentary we seek to avoid. Instead of being frustrated, simply descend again to the water's depths. There you will find God graciously waiting, even when you do not sense it.

Many in the contemplative tradition have described the experienced of a scattered prayer life as "monkey mind." Like monkeys in a tree, our thoughts jump from branch to branch. Goleman asserts "The inner tug to drift away from effortful focus is so strong that cognitive scientists see a wandering mind as the brain's 'default' mode— where… the ability to stay steady on one target and ignore everything else operates in the brain's prefrontal regions."[47] Once we begin to identify this occurrence, it is best to name it and return again to the depths. The 20th century Serbian monk, Elder Thaddeus of Vitovnica believed,

> the mind is a great wanderer. It is always traveling. It cannot rest until the only One who can lay it to rest appears… And so, this means that our mind cannot attain peace unless the Mighty One, the Hol Daniel Goleman y Spirit, enlightens us. That is when our minds learn to contemplate in the right way, and we come to the realization that quiet and

---

47. Goleman, Daniel (2013-10-08). Focus: The Hidden Driver of Excellence (p. 15). HarperCollins. Kindle Edition.

gentle thoughts, full of love and forgiveness, are the way to peace and stillness.[48]

Diving into the depths of God's ocean is one of the most difficult modes of prayer. We are programmed to produce, and sitting with God doesn't usually feel very productive, particularly when one first begins centering prayer. However, this practice imparts immense joy over time as we discover that God is not after our production. To be sure, life in Christ does bear fruit, but only after receiving proper watering and exposure to the light that brings it into season.

Practice

Set your alarm for eighteen minutes. Imagine yourself as a diver in the sea. Now descend to the depths, connect your breath with your word, and practice centering prayer using the four R's below.

1) <u>Resist</u> no thought: don't try too hard not to think because that will cause you to think.

2) <u>Retain</u> no thought: let thoughts go like an object that floats into a net and then escape to the other side.

---

48. Smiljanic, Ana (2013-11-11). Our Thoughts Determine Our Lives: the Life and Teachings of Elder Thaddeus of Vitovnica (Kindle Location 723). St. Herman of Alaska Brotherhood. Kindle Edition.

3) <u>React</u> to no thought: Again, don't get caught up in reacting to your monkey brain. Let it go.

4) <u>Return</u> to your sacred word.

6

GAZE

You shall gaze upon many things beyond telling, and you shall hear extraordinarily more things, which you cannot express with your tongue.
-Saint Symeon, the New Theologian

When You Know You're Known

Elaina and I met at a coffee shop in Westwood, California. A friend of ours connected us because she was in search of a church, and having just moved there myself, I was in search of parishioners. Everybody wins. Within five minutes of conversation I knew I had met my wife. While she went to the restroom I called my sister: "Rebecca, I just met my wife." She replied, "Surely this can't be my brother."

I had previously informed my friends of my resolve to wait a year into the church plant to date anyone. Plans change. I wouldn't recommend dating all those interested in joining your church plant, but we quickly fell for each other; total victims of Cupid.

For the first several months of our relationship we talked, and talked, and talked. We would stay up into the wee hours of the night steeped in conversation both shallow, deep and everywhere in between. I would then begin the drive from her place in Santa Monica back to mine in Long Beach around 3am. This is perhaps the only hour of the day when the 405 freeway offers smooth sailing.

The first stages of any relationship are exciting. Exploring the possibilities of someone's life, discovering another's longings, and discerning your level of commitment to the relationship is processed largely through verbal communication in the initial stages. Conversely, I think this is what scares many about a lifelong marriage commitment:

"What if we run out of things to say?"

"What if I'm not interested in her/him at 50 like I was when I was 30?"

To answers these questions in the order presented – 1. words are the beginning but not the apex of relational intimacy and 2. humans are dynamic and not static entities. We are always changing. What is true on a cellular level is also true on the developmental level. Therefore, we can affirm the statement of Heraclitus of Ephesus with a fair amount of anthropological certainty: *you can never step into the same river twice*. People are like a river who undergo continuous change. The only way you can wake up disinterested in your spouse at the age of 50 is if you stop being curious about who they are becoming. Similarly, although God doesn't change like humans, God is mysterious, and contemplative prayer is a pathway into further intimacy with the Divine.

Those who have crossed the threshold of marriage and find themselves celebrating their 40th wedding anniversaries will tell you that the deepest relational intimacy comes after we run out of words. It is one level of intimacy to look into the depths of another's eyes and wonder what they might say next. It is a deeper level to look into another's eyes and know you are known beyond words. This, I suggest, is the same in our prayer lives. Certainly, we need words – intercession, thanksgiving, adoration and confession. However, the conversation with God has only just begun when we finish talking. For too long I assumed that the conversation with God was over when I ran out of things to say.

Pause for a moment, and let this sink in: God is eternally available. For someone as self-preoccupied as me, it is a marvel that whenever I want to get off "project self" and connect with God, I am met with Divine communion. To answer Philip Yancey's great question, this is what is so amazing about grace! As previously stated in the introduction, every moment of every day the most significant happening in the entire universe is the radical availability of God's Presence. Yet, in almost every moment of every day we remain unaware of this generous gift.

These past few years I have discovered the intimacy of silence. And this silence is not a void, but a place inhabited by a Presence – a Presence that is infinite and available to dwell within me in the form of wordless, accusation-less communion. In the silence we meet God's gaze and experience acceptance, approval, and the joy of being personally and fully known.

From a human-to-human perspective, this is the moment when it is beautiful to sit across the table and simply be together. It represents a depth of intimacy rather than a lack. Words are welcomed, but not essential. Our relationship with God is no different.

For many reasons, most avoid relating to the Divine in this way. Marjorie Thompson cites, "an eighteenth-century priest who once asked an aged peasant what he was doing during the hours and hours he spent sitting in the chapel. The old man replied, 'I look at Him, He looks at me, and we are happy.'"[49] This is spirituality at its zenith. What we discover when we gaze at the Lord in silent prayer is that He is gazing back at us.

Carlo Carretto, the Italian activist claimed, "true prayer demands that we be more passive than active; it requires more silence than words, more adoration than study, more concentration than rushing about, more faith than reason."[50] One cannot help but think of the Virgin Mary as the premier example of this posture. When greeted by the angel she treasured the mystery in her heart. She recognized that God's gift of love had come upon her. She did not earn the gift by religious activity, for if she had, it would no longer be a gift. She passively received God's plan

---

49. Thompson, Kindle Locations 723-724.
50. Carretto, Kindle Locations 637-639.

for her life and treasured the relationship that was growing within her.

Do you realize this Presence lives inside of you? For those in Christ, the Divine Presence housed inside of Mary for nine months is the same Presence that dwells inside of you for the rest of your life. Jesus, according to John, affirmed "we (meaning the Trinity) will come and make our home with her/him."[51] God is closer than breath. And we are invited to participate beyond talking at/with God. We are invited into a gaze.

> But do we really believe this?
> Less active, more passive
> Less words, more silence
> Less study, more adoration
> Less reason, more faith

Do you know anybody who practices this spiritual pathway? Martin Laird remarks in, *The Sunlit Absence*,

> Our five senses, along with the discursive (or thinking) mind, deal with objects (whether conceptual or physical objects) and are predisposed to and preoccupied with feeling, thinking, perceiving, language, stimulation, and feedback. But God is not an object in the way these things are objects. God

---

51. John 14:23.

cannot be grasped the way other things are grasped by our normal ways of knowing and perceiving.[52]

Truly, as we grow in prayer, which is to say, as we grow up in our relationship with God, prayer becomes less something we do and more a way of being with God.[53] Theology helps us form categories for the relationship, but theology is not the relationship. Mission is the fruit of our relationship with God, but is not the relationship. Prayer is not one of many functions in your relationship with God; prayer *is* your relationship with God. And for many, this is a challenging idea. We much prefer being devoted churchgoers, active missionaries and astute theologians. The reason for this preference is that these endeavors tap deeply into our egos, which take pride in producing as the essence (rather than the fruit) of our spirituality. Those activities align with our habitual modes of controlling our performance to achieve an objective. We are far more comfortable with striving.

This way of prayer, the gaze, is difficult to learn, no doubt. However, once one pushes through the initial "boredom" and beyond the introductory phases of stillness, reducing prayer to cataphatic "conversations" becomes dissatisfying. You discover what you previously settled for in prayer no longer brings a fulfilling level of intimacy. In the silence we meet grace not in a doctrine but in the person of Jesus. Again, Laird sums it well:

---
52. Laird, 91.
53. Ibid., 92.

the senses must learn to abide in stillness. But because we are accustomed to so much stimulation, our initial encounters with deeper levels of stillness tend to register as boredom or deprivation of something that we think should be there. With time and perseverance this stillness will register differently, not as boredom, but as a free-flowing vastness and liberating peace that has no opposite, and so embraces all opposites, both boredom and zeal. In this silent land we are taught gradually to "walk by faith and not by sight" (2 Cor 5:7).[54]

Furthermore, the 20th century Swiss Theologian, Hans Urs Von Balthasar, claimed "the longer one gazes into this mystery, the more one longs to go on gazing, glimpsing the fulfillment of that to which our entire creaturely nature aspires."[55] Gazing, therefore, into God becomes the longing we sensed, but could never articulate. And the reason we could not articulate it is precisely because words are inadequate to broker the kind of depth God longs for us to experience. The mystery of his infinite nature is enough to occupy our curiosity for a lifetime until we see him face to face.

Action

At a cursory glance, an often employed but misguided critique of this method of prayer is ostensibly its private

---

[54] Ibid., 91.

[55] Hans Urs von Balthasar, Prayer, trans. Graham Harrison (San Francisco: Ignatius, 1986), 24.

nature. The same critique is often doled out to monks who are misperceived as people seeking to escape society while seeking solitude. However, this is far from being true. In the latter, monks generally retreat to the outskirts of the city in order to gain emotional and spiritual "altitude" to properly intercede for it. Further, monks are steeped in community as a way of life. Similarly, the contemplative method of prayer is designed to bring security, freedom and capacity for the Christian to engage the world.

Henri Nouwen wrote of the trajectory of Jesus' ministry as always moving in a linear format from solitude to community to ministry. Truly, the day begins in our inner room, both crying out (cataphatic) and gazing (apophatic) with God. The resource of prayer is designed to lead us to see others and respond in light of the Kingdom of God. The intimacy we experience inwardly through contemplation eventually manifests outwardly through action, and this action reflects the work that is being done in us while we gaze upon our God. That said, we must be careful to wield contemplation for production purposes. Yet, it is clear from the ministry of Jesus that this kind of inward intimacy with the Father, through the Son, in the Spirit produces fruit. We don't have to focus on the results, but the seed scattered into the soil of our praying souls will super/naturally birth love toward our neighbor.

As we awaken to greater self-awareness, we also awaken to awareness of the needs of others. Instead of being engulfed in the noise and distractions of modern life, contemplation gives us the necessary resources to see and hear ourselves and others. If it doesn't then most likely you have yet to move into spiritual contemplation. As we embrace the image of God within ourselves (which is always graced and never earned), we see that God has graced everyone with this same image, even those who have yet to receive the Spirit through the confession of Christ as Lord. And we glorify God as we honor God's image in everyone we encounter.

May you experience God within. And as you experience more and more of this divine, eternal availability, may you become the blessing this world is waiting for. As a result of this, may you testify to the veracity of Isaiah's prophetic cry, "by waiting and calm you shall be saved; in quiet and trust lies your strength."

PRACTICE

As you are becoming more adept at centering prayer, set the timer to twenty minutes. Most contemplatives recommend twenty minutes as the minimum time needed to truly enter into the depths of the self and discover God. After twenty minutes we finally experience release from all the noise and can rest with God. Practicing the four R's, begin by retrieving your sacred word and sit for twenty minutes. Record the experience in your journal.

Bibliography

Appleton, George. *The Oxford Book of Prayer*. Oxford [Oxfordshire]: Oxford University Press, 1985.

Augustine, Scholastica Hebgin, and Felicitas Corrigan. *St. Augustine on the Psalms*. Westminster, Md: Newman Press, 1960.

Balthasar, Hans Urs von. *Prayer*. New York: Sheed & Ward, 1961.

Bonhoeffer, Dietrich, and Jana Riess. *God Is on the Cross: Reflections on Lent and Easter*. Louisville, Ky: Westminster/John Knox Press, 2012.

_____*Life Together*. New York: Harper & Row, 1954.

Bourgeault, Cynthia. *Centering Prayer and Inner Awakening*. Cambridge, Mass: Cowley Publications, 2004.

Carretto, Carlo. *Letters from the Desert*. Maryknoll, N.Y.: Orbis Books, 1972.

Goleman, Daniel. *Focus: The Hidden Driver of Excellence.* 2013.

Harrington, Daniel J. *The Gospel of Matthew.* Collegeville, Minn: Liturgical Press, 1991.

Holder, Arthur G. *Christian Spirituality: The Classics.* London: Routledge, 2009.

Jensen, L. Paul. *Subversive Spirituality: Transforming Mission Through the Collapse of Space and Time.* Eugene, Or: Pickwick Publications, 2007.

Laird, M. S. *A Sunlit Absence: Silence, Awareness, and Contemplation.* New York: Oxford University Press, 2011.

Mulholland, M. Robert. *The Deeper Journey: The Spirituality of Discovering Your True Self.* Downers Grove, Ill: IVP Books, 2006. Nouwen, Henri, *Moving from Solitude to Community to Ministry*, http://www.leadershipjournal.net. 1995, 81.

Nouwen, Henri J. M. *The Genesee Diary: Report from a Trappist Monastery.* Garden City, N.Y.: Doubleday, 1976.

_____. *Moving from Solitude to Community to Ministry*, http://www.leadershipjournal.net. 1995, 81.

Sittser, Gerald Lawson. *Water from a Deep Well: Christian Spirituality from Early Martyrs to Modern Missionaries.* Downers Grove, Ill: IVP Books, 2007.

Tadej, and Ana Smiljanic. *Our Thoughts Determine Our Lives: The Life and Teachings of Elder Thaddeus of Vitovnica.* Platina, CA: St. Herman of Alaska Brotherhood, 2009.

Teresa, and Mirabai Starr. *The Interior Castle.* New York: Riverhead Books, 2003.

Thibodeaux, Mark E., and Mark J. Link. *Armchair Mystic: Easing into Contemplative Prayer.* Cincinnati, Ohio: St. Anthony Messenger Press, 2001.

Thompson, Marjorie J. *Soul Feast: An Invitation to the Christian Spiritual Life.* Louisville, Ky: Westminster John Knox Press, 1995.

Additional Resources for Various Occassions

Group Study –
Centering Prayer and Inner Awakening, Cynthia Bourgeault
The Naked Now, Richard Rohr

Devotional Meditations –
Beginner: *Common Prayer*, Shaine Claiborne
Intermediate: *On the Threshold of Transformation*, Richard Rohr
Advanced: *New Seeds of Contemplation*, Thomas Merton

Personal Equipping –
The Sunlit Absence, Martin Laird
Merton's Palace of Nowhere, James Finley
Open Mind, Open Heart, Thomas Keating

Historical Perspectives –
Christian Spirituality: The Classics, Arthur Holder
Waters from a Deep Well, Gerald Sittser

Made in the USA
Lexington, KY
21 June 2016